BY MC LYTE AND LYNN RICHARDSON

A FUN AND FAVORABLE GUIDE TO GETTING AND KEEPING A RELATIONSHIP.

YOUR MAN & YOUR MONEY

HOW TO GET'EM AND HOW TO KEEP'EM

Requests for permission and other inquiries should be addressed to:

Publisher:	Sunni Gyrl, Inc.
Publisher Address:	14431 Ventura Blvd #120
Publisher City, State, Zip:	Sherman Oaks, CA 91423
Website:	www.sunnigyrl.com
Phone:	855.MCLYTE1
ISBN 13:	978-0-9773232-6-5

Web / Social Media
URL:	www.yourmanandyourmoney.com
Youtube:	www.yourmanandyourmoney.tv
Facebook / IG:	@YourManAndYourMoney
Twitter:	@YourManAndMoney

"More money doesn't solve a man problem and a man can't solve a money problem.

But with the right man in her life, any woman can achieve harmony in both."
Dr. Lynn Richardson

What's Inside

Your Man

Lynn: With social media and all of the technology available today, how do you date in the 21st century?

Lyte: Very carefully!! Lol. I was single for a long time before I met the man that I'm with and I was pretty much scared to make any kind of move. I asked God to make a way out of no way. I gave up looking for who I thought was right for me and left it to Him. See, when I was looking for myself I was a complete mess. All I know is I came out of all that tragedy knowing that all that looks good, ain't good.

It was clear to me that I was looking for love in all the wrong places and getting nowhere fast. I started to look at the clock and it was indeed moving quickly. During the time I was searching, I had two very distinct groups of friends. The first group decided to marry early or at least they were in committed relationships and they all had kids. They were either flourishing as a couple or they were completely bitter about having spent all of their 20s and 30s raising kids and tending to their families. I guess the grass always looks greener on the other side and they somehow figured that the single folks without children were free and happy. Well, I can honestly say that certainly was not true for me. I was not happy being single. I wanted the companionship of a man to come home to at night and someone I could share my life with. It's all about timing I presume. Settling down takes courage. Right there, right then at that point when you decide to settle down, you are committing to be there for the long haul and to take responsibility. I heard someone say when it comes to finding a companion, you find a reflection of yourself, and I wasn't anything worth finding at that time, so I knew I needed work.

Then there was the other group that decided to do everything late in life...well I'm not so sure they planned it that way, but that's the way it turned out. Many of them are still single trying to find the love of their life. Only great thing about that is that they haven't given up: I was in that group.

I began to take a deeper look into why I was single and what I had done or was still doing to perpetuate this state of single hood. The truth was I just needed to let it all go. I needed to be freer and not walk with the expectation of what he was going to look like, sound like or act like. I had to reevaluate my list of desires because what I was asking for was completely coming from a place of ego. Once I let all that go, I could actually hand it over to GOD and let him take charge.

Living in California didn't prove to be an easy state to date in as an African American woman.

At some point I had to seek the counsel of GOD. I had done it all by myself up until then and I wasn't getting anywhere. I decided to use the technology we have today to open myself up to dating in a different way. I thought if the aesthetics were removed from the scenario, I'd get to really know him before anything else. I'd have a deeper appreciation for him. In addition, being a celebrity can sometimes hinder meeting new people and it certainly presents challenges when it comes to meeting a man who could be a great dating candidate. So I actually took advantage of the online dating sites – I thought I could meet someone there, just like I could meet someone anywhere – and I continued to pray about the man God had set aside for me.

Lynn's Thoughts:

First, I guess you can meet a man anywhere, including the internet. It goes without saying, however, that when there is no mutually known trusted party involved (like a friend introducing you to her colleague), then safety is an issue. If you want to see someone past the first group date alone, then you need to do a background check. A man who has nothing to hide and is really interested won't mind.

Second, since Demietrius and I have been married for decades and I haven't dated since the 90's, I realize many things have changed on the dating scene – texting, communicating, etc. – but some things need to stay the same. I have a problem with some of the ways technology is used in the relationship game as a whole. You can't teach an old woman new tricks and I don't believe you can give an age-old process – dating and courting – a complete facelift. If I was dating in the 21st century, a man would NOT be able to have a whole conversation with me via text during the "getting to know you" and "I'm head over heels in love with you" stages of dating. I have seen my daughters and others carry on multiple conversations with multiple different people about different topics at the same time via text! And don't get me started on the men. They're sending body parts and all kinds of foolishness via text. I believe two people who are interested in each other should take the time to TALK to each other. That's the way it's been since the beginning of time. And that's the way it should stay.

Third, fellas (let's just pretend I'm dating, and we know I'm not because I'm in love with Demietrius) -- don't text me and ask me if you can call. Call me. I may answer and I may not. The anticipation of waiting for a woman to call back would keep the right man curious enough to stay engaged. If I tell him he can call, well that's just too easy. There still needs to be a chase involved and the guy should do the chasing. The Bible says when a man finds a wife, he finds a good thing. Moral of the story here: let him chase you (but don't run too long, lol!).

Lynn: What was your first impression about your man?

Lyte: In all honesty, the first time I saw him was in a photo online. I never thought I'd live to tell the story that I found my "soul mate" on "Match." I had a few friends that had some success online with dating, but then I also had a few that said it wasn't worth the trouble. Well I took my chances anyway and went out on a few dates in the beginning; but there was nothing to write home about.

Lynn: Oh no, sister! You're not gonna skip right over the "online" guy who came to visit and we discovered he was an undercover abuser after the second date and the one who

went off on you because you wouldn't come up to his hotel room and the one who turned psycho because you had to cancel your date when you hurt your back and the one who kept name dropping when he found out you were really MC Lyte and the one who . . .

Lyte: Ok! LOL! You are crazy!

Lynn: No, THEY were crazy! I will admit that I was on the verge of catching a case a few times. The only thing worse than a woman scorned is her crazy sister! LMBO!

Lyte: LOL. Yes, those were bad apples. But back to my love. When I first saw a photo of him online I thought: I like his smile and his eyes looked genuine. I read his profile and he was from upstate NY and that right there peaked my interest. It's a real pill trying to date here on the west coast. Nearly everyone has an angle and it gets really tired really soon. Aside from that, as you know, I have this special kind of humor that takes a special type of person to understand. Being from New York, my pace is a bit fast for LA and I needed someone who understood that. On top of all that, his photos looked like he enjoyed laughing and having a good time.

Meeting him in person, he just had this huge smile that wouldn't stop. NO, I mean literally, he wouldn't stop smiling so I thought ok, what's wrong here? I thought for a second he was kidding me, but the truth is you can't fake good energy. He was so pleasant and relaxed. My first impression was, when will I see him again?

Lynn: What do you love about your man?

Lyte: I love that we could laugh together. Initially I was on tour for several months so we spent a substantial amount of time learning about each other over the phone, so I agree with you that text-talking is not really cool. The first time we talked was for about 5 hours and the next day was the same. For the entire week, we clocked about 6 hours a day of talk time and it never seemed like enough. I knew that by putting in that kind of time, he was committed to getting to know me and he was committed to doing whatever it took to stay connected. I loved that not even time or distance could stop us. We talked about everything and anything. We laughed but we also had emotional moments when talking about people, places and things that affected us in deep ways.

Lynn: How did the actual relationship part start?

Lyte: Well, it started because he stayed connected. It flowed. He understood my rhythm. I loved that he was thoughtful and that he treated me like a woman. Wait, let me rephrase that, of course, all men have treated me like a woman, but this was different. Most of my relationships had stemmed from great friendships, where we decided, "hey let's try this relationship thing." Nevertheless, my good guy friends would never put on the bells and whistles with all the romantic courtship that I love. My guy now opens and closes doors for me and cares for me in a way that makes me feel loved as his significant other and not just his best friend.

He visited me a few times on the road and as a result of spending time together, we realized rather quickly that neither of us would be happy without the other. It was really that easy in acknowledging the power of love, and you just don't find it everywhere, every time.

One day while in Chicago he came to visit, and when I went to introduce him to a cast member,

20

I was stuck with not knowing what to call him. He was so much more than a friend, I couldn't very well reduce the introduction to that. I didn't want to say 'boyfriend' when he and I hadn't had that discussion. I waited for us to talk and asked his thoughts on the matter and he reminded me of something he had asked me weeks prior. He had asked was I ready and I guess at that point I wasn't because the question itself escaped me.

We were now moving into a new space, one that required transparency and admittance that love had hit us both and we were ready to experience one another in a real and true way.

I loved that before his Grandmother passed, he made sure she was comfortable. He loved her and didn't mind doing whatever it took to make her feel whole and loved. I loved that he had a beautiful relationship with his sister and how loving they were towards one another. He didn't mind sharing his knowledge and providing leadership for all his siblings.

I love his optimism and his positive attitude about life, love and business. He's a go getter and I love his energy around wanting to succeed. He's a God fearing man and that's a must have.

It was almost like we knew within the first phone call that we were on to something incredibly special. We decided within the first 2 weeks that we wanted to really give us a solid try and that meant starting a relationship that would be exclusive. We didn't want any outside distractions deterring us from really getting to know one another.

Quite frankly, it was growing increasingly awkward when introducing him as just his name with no title of any kind: not a boyfriend, not a friend, not anything – so weird. That's really what sparked the conversation for us and once we started to talk about it, we quickly realized we were already in a relationship; we just hadn't called it anything.

Lynn's Thoughts:
Aweeeee, this is so sweet! Demietrius and I met at my friend's house. She had been telling

me about him and vice versa and I was interested in meeting him. So she called one day and said "Be at my house in fifteen minutes because Demietrius will be here in a few minutes." So I waited thirty minutes and when I got there, he wasn't there! I was hot! I didn't want it to look like I was there waiting for him. I wanted him to be waiting for me, lol! So he got there a few minutes later, she introduced us, and I knew he was my husband. Girl I was looking cute too! My hair was in a fresh bob and my makeup was on point. But I couldn't let him know I was too interested. A few months earlier he had called me while he was still dating someone and I hung up on him. I was not playing that game. LOL! So I kept it cool. He called me a few days after we met at my friend's house (I don't know what took him so long) and it's been 23 years. ☺

Our first official date was at my apartment and I cooked dinner: hamburgers and french fries and it was sooooooo good! We went grocery shopping together and I'm not sure if we talked a lot or if it was just me talking a lot, LOL, but I knew I was comfortable with him, I felt safe with him, and I could easily love him.

Lynn: What's the worst advice your mother gave you when it comes to men?

Lyte: If it's too hard, let it go. That was bad advice. I've learned if you want anything that's worth having, you have to be prepared to work hard to get it and keep it. Of course this stands true for relationships, but it also rings true for friendships, work and your spiritual walk. There will be times when it feels like walking away would just rectify it all, but I quickly learned nothing of significance is ever built with that mind frame. People are dynamic, situations aren't always transparent, sometimes you have to go deep and see what's beyond the surface and guess what? None of that is easy. It all proves to be difficult at one point and that's when you make the decision to stay engaged and keep moving the dial or you give in and quit, like so many others.

Lynn: What's the best advice your mother gave you when it comes to men?

Lyte: My mother taught me to never ever, ever take any wooden nickels. That meant never let the wool be pulled over my eyes. She felt that it was really important for me to know there were gamers out there and if I weren't careful, I'd be a victim. Being a survivor of domestic abuse, my mom made certain to instill the will to know an abuser when I saw him. She also taught me matters of the heart matter the most and it didn't matter if he didn't make a lot of money or have material items, as long as he loved me, had potential and put forth the effort to make me happy and make our relationship successful.

She also shared that if and only if a man loves his mother, can he love you. She was and is all about being happy and making sure a relationship adds to your happiness and doesn't take away. She always said, tell your man the truth and nothing could ever come back and haunt you. It may not have everyone feeling great in the beginning, but soon after, understanding, respect and trust will make it all worth the effort.

Lynn's Thoughts:
No one really shared advice with me, but I saw things and heard stories that helped me draw my own conclusions. My mother was a victim of domestic violence, so I knew at a young age that I would not be with any man who was mean to me. My grandmother, who raised me, was a firecracker! She told me how she stood

up to her husband who was an alcoholic and how she ultimately left the marriage, with an eighth grade education, three kids to raise and no financial support, so she could save her life and so she wouldn't have to take his! That showed me strength and courage. I knew as a young child that I would be more like my grandmother and less like my mother in a relationship.

But my grandmother did give me a bit of bad advice. She told me, regarding money, "what's his is mine and what's mine is mine." LOL! Haven't we all heard that one? I honestly don't think that's fair. I understand that the women of her generation had different circumstances, but in the 21st century, I believe transparency is best in relationships. I don't believe I should have a hidden account and I don't want my man to have one either. I have my views about joint and separate accounts, which I will share later, but I don't want to do anything in a relationship that I don't want done to me. So, I guess I'm standing against a tradition that many women still hold today. But not only am I married, I am HAPPILY AND JOYFULLY married . . . so I think I will stick to what my heart says on this one.

Lynn: What is the best thing you did for yourself to prepare for a healthy relationship with your man?

Lyte: I gave it GOD. But before I could even ask God to get involved, I had to do my part. I had to get rid of all of my old baggage – junk that was holding me back. I had to clean house of old flings, those hanging on and back biters. I had to check myself and ask what kind of man did I really want in my life and after that I had to become what I wanted to find. All the qualities I wanted in him, I had to be sure I possessed them too, which meant I had to free myself of the belief that I wasn't good enough. I was truly insecure about what I had to give. I wasn't confident that it would be enough and because of that, I attracted men who were insecure about what they had to offer.

I became strong, knowing that what I had to offer was special, beautiful and needn't be compared to anyone at all. I asked God to make me whole with the gifts He had given to me and no one else. He made me aware of all the qualities I possessed and had to offer. Listening is the best. Listening to your man, yes, but listening to GOD is a whole 'nother situation. Also, absorbing loving words from a circle of wisdom comprised of women who have had successful relationships was a good thing. It's always good to talk to someone who has not only been where you are, but who actually knows where you are going. In other words, I want advice from people who have not just walked it, but from someone who got to the finish line. I want advice from empirical experience, not just a hypothetical point of view.

Lynn's Thoughts:

My heart was broken at an early age and it nearly destroyed me, so I vowed that it would never happen again. First, I healed, and then I chose to love again. I did not let the first breakup keep me from believing love was possible; that's the main reason I think I've been in a happy and drama-free marriage for over 20 years: I believed. That was the best preparation. In addition to that, I didn't settle! If a guy was 20 minutes late and didn't have the decency to call, I was no longer available! I had minimum non-negotiable principles and I believed that the man for me – and the man for any woman who is true to herself – would respect and actually appreciate my boundaries and standards. I'm a firm believer that men will do whatever you allow them to do in most cases, so it's up to us as women to determine what we will accept.

But it didn't stop with me. I set standards for the other men around me. I did not allow my brother or cousins to come to my house with one woman after the next. If they did, I would have had no problem embarrassing them: "I'm sorry ma'am, he was just in here yesterday with somebody else!" LOL! Laughing but totally serious. Minimum standards and belief in the best are key to establishing any healthy relationship. I did not want to see the men in my life treating any woman the way I would not want a man to treat me or my daughter or mother or sister.

Lynn: Which famous couple do you model your union after and why?

Lyte: I'd like to look back and feel as accomplished in my relationship as Michelle and Barack Obama. They've got that long lasting love that no thing or no one can interrupt. They've built an empire, raised 2 queens and inspired the world – all while loving and holding each other up. Like Michelle, I want to be the backbone that gives my husband the support that's needed to keep him uplifted. I can only imagine the talks they have that help maintain the bond and the amazing amount of trust that exists between the two. I'd like my husband to adore me as Barack does his wife. I also understand that there isn't a relationship under the sun that can blossom without care and attention. You get out what you put in and it's clear those two have worked really hard to be where they are in the world and with one another.

Just as I may look to many famous couples for inspiration, I also look at ordinary every day couples who exemplify extraordinary love. I love asking questions. I've gotten the best advice from those who aren't necessarily famous. Will Smith once shared that I should just be the light. Be the light that the man in my life can't get enough of. He also said, when it's all said and done, that a man just wants to feel safe, needed and loved.

Lynn: Which famous couple DON'T you want to be like and why?

Lyte: I don't want to be like Alec Baldwin and Kim Basinger or OJ and Nicole. I want to feel safe in a relationship and these women were abused and had to fight for their lives repeatedly. That's not love; more importantly, living in fear is something we should steer clear of. NO relationship is worth your self-esteem, your self-respect . . . your life.

What I don't want to be is the woman who's so scared to be alone that she accepts love from anyone. I see plenty of women in the entertainment business who are so afraid that their knight in shining armor isn't coming that they settle for the wolf in sheep's clothing. I see famous men who have chosen the wrong woman to be vulnerable with, had their heart broken, and now they are too scared to give of themselves so all they do now is take - take - take.

Lynn's Thoughts:
I like the example set by Ossie Davis and Ruby Dee. They married in their twenties, worked together their entire lives, and stayed together for 57 years – when Ossie passed at the age of 87. What a legacy. Of course, I love the Obamas too. I love their sense of family and I appreciate and personally understand that they make decisions with their children in mind; Michelle Obama seemed to be the

steadfast center of the children's wellbeing in the midst of the ultimate public life and I believe President Obama loved her even more for that. I believe a good man respects, loves and appreciates a great woman and a good wife. I believe he honors, with a deep sense of reverence, the principles of a great mother.

I can think of a boatload of couples I would not want to emulate. While I empathize with and do not judge them, I do not take lightly the example set at least in the public eye of what NOT to do. Ike and Tina Turner stand out. What appeared to be domestic abuse and the pressures of entertainment were indeed a recipe for disaster. They were a public example of many millions of lives we never see publicly. I pray that people will love themselves enough to never allow themselves to be publicly humiliated in that way and I pray that abusers receive the healing they need to feel good enough about themselves so that they will not feel the need to hurt others.

Lynn: Do you like spending time with your man's friends and family?

Lyte: Because all of his family lives back east, I haven't had much time with them all, but I have met them. We visited his Grandparents on the east coast and they were beautiful people. Generally speaking, because I grew up in a household with just my mom and I, I love being in the company of a big family. I love the laughter and chatter, the kids and the activity. I look forward to spending more time with his family for sure.

Lynn: How often do you talk on the phone with your man?

Lyte: We talk each and every day. Some days we may speak for longer periods of time when and if time allows.

We do a great deal of talking over the phone throughout each day when I' m traveling so we maintain a strong connection until we see each other again. We really enjoy one another's company and that leads us to really want to be a part of each other's lives. I love calling him with good news or maybe even something that's made me feel uneasy. He calls me for quick strategy sessions or to share something that has occurred in his day.

When you like who you love it makes life a whole lot easier. We laugh and when we're done laughing with one thing, we laugh some more. We both take life as it comes and stay pretty evenly keeled, so we're always open to talking about things as they happen.

Lynn: How often do you think of your man when he's not around?

Lyte: All the time! We are definitely connected because we're often thinking about each other at the same time. He'll call and seconds prior I'd have him on my mind. I think about him when I think of my future. I think of him when I want to share things that have happened throughout my day. I think of him before I make certain decisions that will inevitably affect us both. I keep him in mind when I'm thinking about scheduling and how it will affect when and where we will see each other. I think of us when I hear a song or an artist that we've spoken about. I think of him when I eat certain foods that I know he has a strong opinion about. I think of him!

Lynn: Do you get each other's feelings without the need to say anything?

Lyte: YES!! It's amazing how we are always on the same page, or at least we have been. He often says, I was just thinking that and I find myself saying that more often than not.

Lynn: Do you share passwords for social media, phones, etc?

Lyte: I'm not married yet, so I'm not so sure how to answer this. Given this day and time . . . (clearing throat) . . . uhmm . . . well, not now. I feel like giving passwords and private information of that nature is to be left to married couples. I, myself, have nothing to hide, but I do feel like sharing passwords to social media, emails and bank accounts is too much for folks who are just dating.

First off, it's an issue of trust and I wouldn't want to ask him for his passwords because it denotes that I haven't any trust, and I do. However, if he saw fit to share his passwords with me voluntarily, that's another situation.

Lynn's Thoughts:
Maybe not in the beginning, but if a man can't share his passwords at some point in the relationship, then he's hiding something. Period. And I'm not interested. I'm not saying "sit down and have a meeting and exchange passwords"; rather, all I'm saying is this: If his phone or my phone is on the table and one of us needs to get the other person's phone for some reason, sharing the password to handle the situation should not be a problem. If it is, then we definitely have a problem. It goes both ways.

Lynn: Do you feel jealous if your man hangs out with a friend of the opposite sex?

Lyte: I wouldn't call it jealousy, but I do have questions: who is she? Where did she come from? Did she appear yesterday? If she's been around how long? Did you have a relationship with her or was there something romantic between you in the past?

Lynn's Thoughts:
He doesn't have any friends that he use to sleep with and neither do I. It's unnecessary. For what? Now there are a few exceptions: in the case of a baby's momma or a baby's daddy, I think it's in the best interest of everyone and the child to be friends. If there is a work

situation, maybe. I'd need to understand the terms of that relationship. It's not about trust, it's about safety and security. I would not want my man feeling unsafe or insecure because I'm always hanging out with my ex-boyfriend who is now my "friend" and vice versa. And I definitely don't think either of us should have friends that the other is uncomfortable with. (except maybe that sister-friend of yours that talks too much, but she's otherwise harmless, lol, laughing but serious, I've had one or two of those – or maybe his boy that he grew up with that refuses to grow up, but your man knows how to keep his boundaries and his priorities in check).

Lynn: Do you forgive your man's mistakes easily?

Lyte: I believe so, especially when he knows whatever he did was a little off. There's nothing like acknowledgement with something like that. If the person can admit to making a mistake and not run from it.

Lynn's Thoughts:
I only forgive them easily if he admits them easily! LOL! I don't understand why men refuse to admit it when they are wrong. Then they wanna call women crazy (which is somewhat true, but that's not the point if they are driving us there!) I mean, since women are right 99.99999999 percent of the time, they

should just admit their transgressions automatically! But their egos won't allow them to! LOL! Seriously though, I don't believe in going to bed angry and in my twenty plus years of marriage, I honestly don't remember too many times when we've done that, maybe once or twice. So yes, I will forgive him easily if he admits his error quickly, but if he doesn't, we're gonna be up allllllll night until he does! LOLOLOL!

Lynn: Which do you do best: Cooking or cleaning for your man?

Lyte: Wow, I wish I could say I love to do it all but that just wouldn't be the truth now would it Lynn? I love cooking, sometimes, lol. I love seeing a smile on his face, not necessarily because the food is so GOOD but because he knows I care enough about him to stop what I'm doing and make sure he's GOOD.

I clean because I like a clean house. I'd clean whether he was there or not. But I have to say he also cleans which makes it great. I hear once you have kids and they get old enough, you don't have to clean ANYthing ANYmore, lol. At least that's what YOU say!

Lynn: Yep! I have three kids who've been cleaning since they were two years old!

Lynn: Which do you like least and why?

Lyte: Cleaning would have to be it. Takes up way too much time. While cleaning I'm thinking about all the other things I need to get done. Sure a housekeeper can come in to do what's necessary for the week, but then it's the day to day that requires immediate attention. I'd be crazy to let things pile up until the housekeeper gets there. Cleaning should be left for those who love to do it.

Lynn's Thoughts:
I love to cook and I use to clean the house, spic and span from top to bottom, every Friday after work before we would go out for the weekend. Then we started having kids! I have always loved to cook, but eventually I became too tired to do it all while raising kids and

working long hours and traveling; and at that point, me doing the cleaning was no longer an option. I had a housekeeper and then when the kids were old enough (yes, as little bitty children, lol) they started cleaning. I feel like this: If you can play with toys and understand games and work electronic equipment, then you can also clean up! My kids have chores (I have the best chores checklist on the planet designed especially for frustrated parents whose kids "forget" what to do), but I also have a housekeeper. No cleaning for me, but if necessary, I will do it because I refuse to have a nasty house. It's not ladylike.

Lynn: What's your advice on finding and keeping a good man?

Lyte: Not too long ago, I couldn't even answer this question because I didn't have a man. OH BUT NOW...the good Lord saw fit to bless me with a man who possesses a beautiful spirit and loves me through and through. My advice on finding a good man would be to get yourself together. A real man is attracted to strength and confidence. Only an insecure man would want an insecure woman because then he knows he can take advantage of her doubt and uncertainty, both of which are born from the dark. A man is drawn to the light, no pun intended, lol. He's living, but he's looking for more life, so as a woman you must be connected to the only life source we know, God.

Keeping him? More of the same: love, light, truth. You must continue to love you and then so will he. What I mean by that is taking care of yourself, prayer and meditation, eating the right foods, taking care of your body, reading the right books. Just because you're loving him doesn't mean you stop loving yourself.

Lynn's Thoughts:
I think the list of priorities has to be in order.
Values and morals are more important than
money and status. That's in finding the RIGHT
relationship AND keeping it. The best advice I
can give in keeping a good relationship is to put
God first and to be honest with yourself. I've
always been a loyal wife but I haven't always

had the proper posture in my relationship. I was bossy – okay I'm still bossy, but in a good way – and I would make decisions without his approval or insight. That was wack. I came to the point that I realized I did not want to wear the pants in my relationship. Moreover, I was not afraid to admit this: I NEED MY MAN! Yes, I believe in women's rights and all of that, but I am not so far gone that I cannot acknowledge that I want AND need my man. He has been my biggest cheerleader, my greatest supporter, my most committed prayer warrior and my protector. Now don't get me wrong, I wouldn't just fall apart without a man in my life, but the truth is this: I'd rather live my life with him and in a committed relationship than move into the state of mind I see so many strong and beautiful sisters in that says "I can do life with or without a man." If that's what you reinforce, then that's what you will get. In the same way, I can do life with or without a lot of money, but I'd rather have a lot of it so I can live and give back in abundance and I'm not afraid to proclaim that. That's exactly how I feel about having a man.

So, I'd say that the best advice I can give on finding and keeping a good man is this:
Forget about the man that you want and focus on positioning yourself to be mature and stable enough for the man that you NEED. I believe you will learn that the man you need, if God sends him to you, is in fact also the man that you WANT.

Journaling Your Way to Love & Prosperity:
Now it's your turn to write: What are YOUR
thoughts about dating in the 21st Century?

Journaling Your Way to Love & Prosperity:
Now it's your turn to write: What's working for you in getting or keeping a relationship and how can you do it better?

Journaling Your Way to Love & Prosperity:
Now it's your turn to write: What's NOT working for you and what do you need to change?

_____

_____

_____

_____

_____

_____

_____

_____

_____

_____

_____

_____

_____

Journaling Your Way to Love & Prosperity:
Now it's your turn to write: What's the best
relationship advice you've received?

_____

_____

_____

_____

_____

_____

_____

_____

_____

_____

_____

_____

_____

_____

Journaling Your Way to Love & Prosperity:
Now it's your turn to write: What's the worst
relationship advice you've received and how
did you recover from it?

Journaling Your Way to Love & Prosperity:

Now it's your turn to write: What couple, famous or not, would you like to model?

_____

_____

_____

_____

_____

_____

_____

_____

_____

_____

_____

_____

_____

_____

Journaling Your Way to Love & Prosperity:
Now it's your turn to write: What couple was a bad example for you and how did it impact your relationship?

_____

_____

_____

_____

_____

_____

_____

_____

_____

_____

_____

_____

_____

Journaling Your Way to Love & Prosperity:
Now it's your turn to write: What have you
contributed to unhealthy relationships now or
in the past?

_____

_____

_____

_____

_____

_____

_____

_____

_____

_____

_____

_____

_____

_____

_____

Journaling Your Way to Love & Prosperity:
Now it's your turn to write: What changes do
you need to make for yourself in order to
create a healthy relationship?

_____

_____

_____

_____

_____

_____

_____

_____

_____

_____

_____

_____

_____

_____

Journaling Your Way to Love & Prosperity:

Now it's your turn to write: Additional thoughts.

_____

_____

_____

_____

_____

_____

_____

_____

_____

_____

_____

_____

_____

_____

Journaling Your Way to Love & Prosperity:
Now it's your turn to write: Additional thoughts.

Your Money: The Plot Thickens

Lynn: How have you felt in the past about making more money than the man you've dated or been in a relationship with?

Lyte: Well, I usually do, so it doesn't feel strange at all. I know money is just a means to make ends meet. Making more money doesn't make me better or smarter or anything. It just says I'm in a position to bring money into manifestation and that position has the ability to change at any moment. God blesses us all with power and sometimes it's in the form of money, so He can bless whoever needs to be blessed through me.

Lynn's Thoughts: I know women who believe that the guy should make more money and they are ONLY interested in men with money. What does "who makes more money" have to do with love, respect, and honesty? More importantly, if money – the man's money in particular — makes the relationship better, then why are there so many rich people who are getting divorced and in unhappy relationships? I think many women grew up with the dream that they would marry a knight in shining armor who would protect them, take care of them, and purchase the biggest house he could find so they could raise their kids behind a white picket fence, but the truth of the matter is this: if they're waiting on a man who has a bigger paycheck than them, they may be waiting forever!

Lynn: Do you believe in maintaining joint checking accounts with your man?

Lyte: I guess I could get used to that. I've never shared an account with anyone so I'll have to hear a good word from the Lord telling me that's what needs to happen. I can probably wrap my head around that once we've decided we're going to marry. I believe once married, it would make sense to have an account that we both contribute to for the household. I actually learned all of this during the Hip Hop Sisters Foundation **Women, W.E.A.L.T.H. and Relationship** panels. It seems like a lot of the women on our panels were into the joint account thing. LOL. It definitely sounds reasonable.

I also believe we should have some sort of savings account so we can prepare for the big moments we'd like to share together.

Lynn's Thoughts:
Okay so my Grandma Bea raised me and like many women, I learned from her: what's his is yours and what's yours is yours. I guess back in those days the man had the account and the woman had nothing. Or maybe they didn't have bank accounts at all, so I understand to some degree. I love my grandmother dearly, she raised me, but I don't really think that's fair

today. I don't want him having a private stash that I don't know about so I don't think I should have one either. I truly believe you should do unto others as you would have them do unto you. So yes, I believe in joint accounts and since Demietrius and I have been married since we were just slightly older than teenagers, everything that we have belongs to both of us. But I guess in the case of twenty-first century relationships wherein two individuals are coming together later in life, it probably makes sense to have a joint account for the bills and separate accounts for individual spending. But I need access to his other accounts. (Demietrius really doesn't want access to mine, but he can certainly have it if he wants). As a matter of fact, he gave me all of his money when we started dating and trusted me to handle all of the bills. I messed things up in the beginning and felt terrible (read "Living Check to Monday"). That taught me to allow him to lead and provide wisdom before making any major financial decisions. Nevertheless, I don't think there should be any money in the relationship that the other doesn't know about or have access to.

Lynn: How do you handle when his family members want to borrow money?

Lyte: Oh my. I guess we could talk about it. Wait, is it from OUR account or just his? LOL! I'd probably want to know how much the family member wanted to borrow and if we could actually gift it rather than loaning it, depending on whether it's a good reason as to why he/she needs it. There has only been one family member in my entire life that has asked to borrow money and believe it or not, it was never returned. I figured that might be the case so the concrete has been laid. She can never ask to borrow money again and as a matter of fact she hasn't and it's been years. Aside from that it's not something that happens as much as I hear others speak about it. OH wait, my Dad! LOL! Well when he calls, I just give it to him but I'm sure once I'm married, there will have to be a discussion if it's to come from our joint account.

Lynn's Thoughts:

The answer is no, usually. But if we want to consider it, then my family members have to ask him and his family members have to ask me. Nobody wants to ask me anything about money because they know it comes with a lecture and I still may not lend them the money afterward! LOL! So it works out.

But seriously, I don't mind giving the money as a gift without the expectation of it being repaid if we discuss it and seek God's counsel. In general, my advice is to never loan money that you can't afford to give away – especially to family members and friends.

Lynn: How do you feel about prenuptial agreements?

Lyte: I used to feel really uneasy about the thought of a prenup, especially as it related to seeing celebrity couples deal with it in a public manner. Take for instance Michael Douglass and his very public prenup with Katherine Zeta Jones. The terms were ridiculous and it felt like the union was one big business deal.

I now have a better understanding of how "out of hand" things can get during a divorce and all of a sudden LOVE is not the common denominator. Halle Berry, Tasha Smith and Regina King are just a few celebrities that have dealt with very public divorces whereby their husbands wanted an exuberant amount of money for spousal support. When I say exuberant, we're talking upwards of twenty thousand to eighty thousand dollars each month. Now this is not my idea of how a man moves on. You would think they would want to fend for themselves and not take a handout from their ex-wives, but that's not the case sometimes. And there's no way to avoid acknowledging how many women have done the same to their wealthy ex-husbands.

A pre-nup can test the strength of a relationship, but I believe if there is true love and transparency, neither party should have an issue with the other wanting to protect their own interest. In fact, if you love someone, you would want to protect them the best way possible.

Lynn's Thoughts:

I think it's a good idea to be clear about assets when two people who have built separate lives come together. However, if you have nothing when you get together and / or you get married young, what's the point? A prenup is not necessary when both parties are starting at ground level.

I do believe, however, that if one party should receive an inheritance, the other person in the relationship should only benefit from that inheritance during the marriage and I believe that the inheritance should remain solely with

the rightful intended heir in the event of a divorce.

Lynn: Would you be interested in being in business with your man?

Lyte: SURE! When I was younger I felt differently because I had seen and heard of such disastrous business relationships that had gone wrong. I heard of so many women who had let their husbands manage them and ended up regretting having made that move. I also heard of couples going into business together and it ending terribly. I imagine it could be a sizable amount of stress working together and attempting to have a household that remains harmonious. While I've seen these types of relationships fail, I've also witnessed them work. Let's take Tamar and Vince for instance, it seems to work for them. He understands her long term goals as an artist and what makes her feel successful. They have a relationship built on trust and love that clearly says the foundation of their relationship reigns supreme over everything.

To be clear, I would be open to the concept of working with my husband. To add even more clarity, I said my husband, not my boyfriend. We would have to completely be on the same page about where we wanted to take the business and also have clearly defined roles and not step on one another's toes.

Lynn: What do you feel about joint or separate ownership of important assets: house, car, business?

Lyte: If I hadn't been mentored by you, I'd say "my name needs to be on everything". I never wanted to have a situation where he moves on and decides to take what's ours because his name is the only one there. Ok, so clearly that comes from watching too many movies, dramas to be specific. I've heard of women getting the ax and having to start their lives all over again. From the bottom up, for real.

I personally believe you should be able to walk away with whatever you put in. I'm all for each individual paying for their own cars because the cost will match their taste.

Lynn's Thoughts:

Here's my advice: get legal advice and don't put all assets in both names. Put the house in one name. Put each car in one name. If you encounter financial difficulty and every asset is in both names, then everyone will be impacted. If however you have the house in one name, the other person can get another house if the first house goes into foreclosure or is upside down and can't be sold. If that house can't be sold, the debt to income ratio could prevent you two from buying a new house, even if you can practically afford it. But if you have the house in one person's name, the

other person can get the new house without facing the red tape of a difficult loan approval. In some states, all property purchased during the marriage or in anticipation of marriage is defined as "marital property" regardless of whose name is on the property. That's how Bernadine got all of that stuff in Waiting to Exhale. In other states, property laws are less liberal.

My other advice is to know your state laws and get an estate plan. Each of you should be properly insured with life insurance policies that will pay off debt and allow the surviving partner to live without the burden of worrying about how to pay for basic living expenses. Long term care insurance will also provide the financial resources needed to care for your loved one in the event that he loses two or more activities of daily living and can no longer care for himself; the same goes for you.

The point here is to get your paperwork in order: an estate plan will dictate what goes to who in the event of death and a prenuptial agreement would outline who gets what in the event of a divorce or separation.

Journaling Your Way to Love & Prosperity:
Now it's your turn to write: What are YOUR thoughts about him making more money? Less money? Joint accounts?

_____

_____

_____

_____

_____

_____

_____

_____

_____

_____

_____

_____

_____

_____

Journaling Your Way to Love & Prosperity:
Now it's your turn to write: What HAS NOT worked for you when it comes to dealing with money in a relationship?

_____

_____

_____

_____

_____

_____

_____

_____

_____

_____

_____

_____

_____

_____

Journaling Your Way to Love & Prosperity:
Now it's your turn to write: What do you need to change in order to make the money situation better in your relationship or perhaps your future relationship?

_____

_____

_____

_____

_____

_____

_____

_____

_____

_____

_____

_____

_____

Journaling Your Way to Love & Prosperity:
Now it's your turn to write: What are your fears about money in a relationship?

_____

_____

_____

_____

_____

_____

_____

_____

_____

_____

_____

_____

_____

_____

Journaling Your Way to Love & Prosperity:
Now it's your turn to write: What money /
relationship experiences have you had that you
want to avoid in the future?

_____

_____

_____

_____

_____

_____

_____

_____

_____

_____

_____

_____

_____

_____

Journaling Your Way to Love & Prosperity:
Now it's your turn to write: What do you need to do consistently to keep Your Man and Your Money in harmony?

_____

_____

_____

_____

_____

_____

_____

_____

_____

_____

_____

_____

Journaling Your Way to Love & Prosperity:
Now it's your turn to write: What are your
additional thoughts about love and money?

Journaling Your Way to Love & Prosperity:
Now it's your turn to write: What are your additional thoughts about love and money?

Real Money Talk: How to Keep It

According to author Pepper Miller in her book "What's Black About It?," African-American females are making the financial decisions in our households more than eighty percent of the time, whether we are married or not, yet we are lagging far behind in the wealth gap, with an average net worth of less than $6,000 according to a recent Pew Hispanic Center report. Even though we may be educated, paid and gifted, the unfortunate truth is that many of us find ourselves not just living check-to-check, but "Living Check to . . . Monday" and a long way from achieving the financial freedom and retirement security we dream of.

With pension plans being virtually obsolete, in most cases, the amount of money we are contributing to our 401k plans will not be enough to sustain our relationships in retirement, so we must find new ways to make sure we will have a "playcheck" when we can no longer work to get a "paycheck." **But how do you do that when you face financial difficulty and if you are living Check to Check as a couple?** How can you save for retirement when the ends aren't meeting and the next payday seems like forever? How do you plan for retirement when you have to pay for your childrens' education?

Well, the first step is this: track your spending. That's right -- each and every penny. Why?

Because some say "money talks," but I say "money walks" away from you quietly and you don't know where it went! In order to find additional money to add to your retirement account, you must get control of your cashflow so you can make better decisions. Here's a great budget to live by - I call it the "10-10-30-50." Every time you and your man get money from any source and for any reason, this is how you should divide it:

10% = Tithing. That's right, tithing is the first nonnegotiable law to achieving abundance. Besides, if you are already broke, then keeping the tithe money doesn't change your situation. So when my back was up against the wall, my husband and I decided to start tithing and when I prayed, I knew that I would at least have God on my broke side!

10% = Saving. You must save in order to prepare for the famine. Statistics show that there have been more millionaires made in the last recession than at any other time in the history of the world! These new millionaires were saving while the rest of us were spending beyond our means and, you guessed, it, Living Check to Monday.

30% = Cash in Your Pocket. This is what you get to spend on all incidentals, like groceries, gas, transportation, lunch, hair, haircuts, nails, electronics and other gadgets, movies, etc. If it doesn't fit in your 30%, then you have to eliminate it! And you must use cash to avoid a spending addiction. Leave your debit card, credit card, and checkbook at home so you can break this terrible addiction that keeps you from being financially free.

50% = Money in Your Checking Account for Bills. Leave 50% in your checking account to pay your bills. If there's not enough money in your account, for your bills, DO NOT, reduce your tithing or saving. You can reduce your 30%, contact your creditors to determine if there are less costly ways to maintain their services, or you can cancel some things all together. Who needs cable when you are living check to Monday? That's what I thought!

The second step? End your spending addiction, which is what you have when you go into a store with the intention of buying toothpaste, but you walk out with one-hundred-seventy-nine-dollars and forty-seven cents worth of stuff you don't need! Or as a couple, you buy too many Christmas presents for your kids who won't even play with those toys more than a few days.

We've all been guilty of overspending at some point, and if we're honest with ourselves, we can all find ways to skim some of our unplanned and/or unnecessary spending and use that money to help build our retirement nest-eggs.

Here are a few tips:

1. End your relationship with coffee shops. Instead, pick up your favorite blend at the grocery store, add your favorite flavored creamer, get generic hot chocolate packets for a rich mocha flavor, and if you absolutely must flaunt like you've actually visited the coffee shop, get the decorated cups at your local discount warehouse. Instead of spending $6 - $10 per day on coffee, you can spend $15 - $20 per month and retain the additional cash to add to your retirement account.

2. Get rid of your landline. Chances are, you and every breathing soul in your household (I'm just waiting for them to come out with

mobile phones for pets!) owns a mobile phone. If you're holding onto you landline for fax purposes, go to your local office supply store and spend the $5 - $7 if and when the need arises. The number of faxes you need to print or send is probably not worth the $600 - $2400 annually per year spent on household landlines.

3. Contact your mobile phone company and negotiate a lower payment. If they tell you that you must be a "new" customer, ask the boss's boss if you need to leave them, cancel your service, then become new again! Chances are, they won't want to lose you as a customer and will find a way to keep your

business and save you a few dollars that you can add to your retirement account.

4. Eliminate your landscaping and/or housekeeping expenses and do the work yourself. Better yet, if you have children (any person who can use an electronic device can also do chores), then they should be making their own beds, doing their own laundry, washing dishes, mopping, vacuuming, and otherwise earning their keep. Seriously, this is a great way to build extra responsibility and add a few extra dollars to the next egg. And do not give them an allowance for doing chores! You are already "allowing" them to live with you! LOL, laughing but VERY serious! Instead, hire

them to work in your home-based business, pay them a fee for doing real work in your very real business, and write the amount that you pay them off on your taxes (consult a tax advisor for more information).

5. If you are a member of any kind of group, club, sorority, or entity that requires regular meetings, end the local coffee house gatherings and conduct the majority of your meetings via conference call. It'll increase the available cash you can allocate towards retirement by ending the sudden-hunger-because-of-the-environment spending, preserve your time and gasoline, and help you keep a few pounds off in the process.

6. Decide who will pay for your children's education and get your kids in on the conversation early. In my house, school is free. After paying for private school for a few years, we decided to choose a neighborhood based on the school system so we would be tuition-free. For college, once again, school is *free*: If they get good grades, they will go to school for free by way of scholarships, and if they don't get good grades, they will go to the *free school*, community college, or whatever and work their way up to the more costly school; either way, it will be *free* to me (and my man, lol!). Most financial experts will advise that you make sure your retirement is on schedule before attempting to fit a college

education in your budget. Kids can get student loans and scholarships, but there are no scholarships for retirement. If you have the extra money to spare, then this is not an issue, but if you are like the millions of people who DO NOT have a lifetime income set for retirement, then rethinking this priority is a major key to financial stability in the long term.

The third step? Start a home-based business so you can **Get Your Money Back** when tax season arrives. The average American only gets about 8 tax deductions (real estate taxes, mortgage interest, charitable donations, and a few others). But if you have a home based business, there are over **440 tax deductions** available to you that you can itemize on Schedule C of your 1040 tax return. One of my clients organizes her college reunion every year. Between site visits, travel, and meals, she spends over $6,000 each year and she never makes a profit. Now that she is in business for herself as an Event Planning Consultant, she gets to write every bit of her class reunion expenses off on her tax return.

How about this: have you ever invited people to your home to eat and have a good time? Well, if you have a home-based business, it's called a business dinner party! Place information about your business near the food. Take pictures of people looking at your business cards. Answer questions about your business and always ask for referrals. When guests ring your doorbell, greet them by saying "How's business?" Get it? I know you do! They may think you're strange, but who cares? As far as I'm concerned, **It's Always Business**, and what's most important, you can write off what you spent on meals, invitations, and other items related to your business dinner party.

And yes . . . it's always business when it comes to the kids too. The IRS allows you to hire your children to work in your home-based business, write off the income you pay them (they don't have to report it unless it's over a certain amount annually), then they can use the money they earn (that you now get to write off) to buy school clothes, school supplies, dance lessons, etc. It's money you would have spent any way, but now, it's a tax write-off. For me, that meant $5,000 times three kids, which was $15,000 in additional tax write-offs each year. And when nieces and nephews and god-children ask for money, I hire them to complete a project in my home-based business, I send them a 1099 at the end of the year and I write that off too!

So, if you haven't done so already, take a look at what you like to do, what you are good at, and/or what you spend your time doing for fun and turn it into a business. Most businesses do not require a license or a tax id number, but check with your local government for registration or permit requirements. In order for your business to be recognized as a business and not a hobby by the IRS, you must have the INTENT on making a profit (you can have a loss) and you must run your business like a business by keeping good records. When you get a receipt, write on the back: who was involved, what you discussed (if it was a dinner meeting), where you were, how much you spent (because receipts fade) and when the event took place. You don't need a receipt for expenses under $75 (unless it's for a hotel room), but I suggest you keep them all anyway. Plus, you should keep a small "tax diary" to record your daily business expense notes and mileage.

Some say this is hard work, but so is being broke! It takes a lot of mental energy when you spend your time robbing Peter to pay Paul; so do the work and remember my mantra, **It's Always Business.** And the good thing is this: my business actually grows as a result, I get to interact with people and have a good time, AND I get my money back during tax season!

The only difference between where you are and where you want to be financially as a couple is the choices you make. Remember the old adage, "a penny saved is a penny earned," and make better decisions with each penny you are blessed to receive so your retirement account will have more than just a few pennies in it when it's time to enjoy the fruit of your labor and love in your latter years.

Journaling Your Way to Love & Prosperity:
Now it's your turn to write: What budgeting
challenges do you have?

Journaling Your Way to Love & Prosperity:
Now it's your turn to write: What items can you get rid of so planning for retirement is possible?

_____

_____

_____

_____

_____

_____

_____

_____

_____

_____

_____

_____

_____

_____

Journaling Your Way to Love & Prosperity:
Now it's your turn to write: Which one of you is better with money and does the other trust that person to lead? Why or why not?

_____

_____

_____

_____

_____

_____

_____

_____

_____

_____

_____

_____

_____

_____

Journaling Your Way to Love & Prosperity:
Now it's your turn to write: Which one of you is better with money and what changes need to be made?

_____

_____

_____

_____

_____

_____

_____

_____

_____

_____

_____

_____

Journaling Your Way to Love & Prosperity:
Now it's your turn to write: What gifts do each of you have that could provide income in a home based business?

_____

_____

_____

_____

_____

_____

_____

_____

_____

_____

_____

_____

_____

Journaling Your Way to Love & Prosperity:
Now it's your turn to write: What can your children do to work in the business and earn an income?

_____

_____

_____

_____

_____

_____

_____

_____

_____

_____

_____

_____

Journaling Your Way to Love & Prosperity:
Now it's your turn to write: What additional thoughts do you have about budgeting and planning for retirement?

Journaling Your Way to Love & Prosperity:
Now it's your turn to write: What do you envision as the ideal retirement for you and your man? Write it & work towards it.

Get Your House In Order: Ask Dr. Lynn

Yes, I mean GET YOUR HOUSE IN ORDER, LITERALLY AND FIGURATIVELY. One of the first steps you and your man will take along the path to building wealth is buying a home. All things considered, it usually makes more sense to own where you live than it does to rent. With that said, I've taken notes and advice from my friends, Attorney Deadra Woods Stokes, credit expert Harrine Freeman, insurance expert Curtis Monday, and financial guru Lori Jones Gibbs, in an effort to provide comprehensive answers to couples looking to buy their first home together.

Q: With all that is going on in the economy, is now a good time to purchase real estate?

A: Yes, now is a great time to purchase real estate, and home ownership is the foundation for building wealth for any couple. Until you own where you live, many other investment vehicles remain out of reach. With homes in many areas at affordable prices, now is a great time to buy at record low prices, hold on to your investment, and receive the tax and other benefits afforded to homeowners. The home you couldn't afford a year or two ago may be in an affordable price range for you today.

Q: What are the steps to buying a home?

A: After you make the decision to build wealth through real estate and become a homeowner, you   should   do   the   following:

Get educated. Taking a home ownership education course will provide you with the general knowledge necessary to get a home, select knowledgeable professionals, and keep your home (avoid and prevent foreclosure). Search for an approved HUD counselor: http://www.hud.gov/offices/hsg/sfh/hcc/hcc_home.cfm.

Get pre-approved. Contact a mortgage professional to determine your approval amount. Suggestion: instead of asking, "How much can we buy?" you should ask "This is how much we can afford to pay monthly for housing, so how much of a home will our pre-determined budget allow us to purchase?" Most real estate agents and down payment programs require a pre-approval prior to working with you.

Get a real estate agent. Work with a local real estate professional who will listen to your desires and help you shop for a home that falls within your price range. Beware! When you start shopping, do not be tempted to "find a way" to buy a home that is more expensive than you can realistically afford. Do not say, "we'll make more money," or "I'll get a second job," etc., etc. Financial stress is the leading cause of failed relationships, so it's best to live below your means then work together to buy a more expensive home when you can really afford it. Some real estate agents may require that you sign a buyer-representation agreement for a mutually agreeable time period. In the event your agent requires you to sign a buyer representation, suggest 30 day increments or less to ensure that the buyer/agent relationship is one that meets your needs. In most cases, a real estate agent should not charge you a fee for buyer

representation (if you are selling a home however, seller paid commissions are usual and customary).

Make your offer. It's a buyer's market and you can offer whatever you like, however keep in mind that the seller has expenses and obligations (mortgage debt to pay off, attorney's fees, etc.) as well, and try to give your highest and best offer during the negotiating process. Ask for any closing cost assistance, known repair requests, and other items you desire at this time. It will be too late to negotiate after your offer is accepted.

Submit your earnest money. If your offer is accepted, you will be required to submit earnest money, preferably in certified funds, to your agent or to the seller's agent. Earnest money is usually $1,000 for average priced existing homes, but is often higher for luxury homes and/or new construction homes. This money is applied to your down payment at the time of closing and is only refundable when certain conditions are met (your loan is denied; there are irreconcilable issues during the attorney review period – please check with your local real estate attorney and the laws in your state).

Attorney review & home inspection. Check with your local real estate attorney, but in most states, there is a five-day attorney review period. You should obtain a home inspection, which will normally take anywhere from 1 ½ hours to 2 hours and will include a detailed overview of the condition of the home and its major systems. During this time, any issues relating to the home inspection, contract terms, and other matters must be addressed; otherwise, the buyer may forfeit certain rights. Please get a real estate attorney. You would not go to a foot doctor for brain surgery, so please be careful when choosing the appropriate attorney to represent you in one of the largest investments you will ever make.

Mortgage Commitment. Your lender will need the contract, proof and source of earnest money, and updated pay stubs, bank statements, and other financial information. You will receive a Good Faith Estimate and a Truth in Lending disclosure which will outline the terms of your loan, interest rate, annual percentage rate, closing costs, and down payment. An appraisal will be ordered to determine the fair market value and general condition of the home (this is separate and distinct from a home inspection). If you are putting down less than

20 percent and the loan requires mortgage insurance, your lender will obtain mortgage insurance at this time. This is not to be confused with homeowners/hazard insurance. You will need to contact your local insurance agent to obtain hazard insurance to protect your home against certain perils like fire, theft, and damage. Finally, after the lender has reviewed all of the above, a Loan Commitment will be issued that will list any additional items required by the buyer or seller prior to closing.

Final Walk Through. Your agent should arrange a final walk-through of the home prior to closing (if you are purchasing new construction, you may need to do several walk-throughs at different phases in the building process). Ensure that any written commitments in terms of repairs have been met and address any outstanding issues with your agent and/or real estate attorney.

Confirm Your Cash to Close. Confirm the final amount you will need to bring to the closing with your lender and/or real estate attorney. Depending on whether or not the closing agent has received all final details from both the buyer and the seller, this may or may not be available. If not, don't panic! Refer to your Good Faith Estimate provided by your lender and bring the amount you need in the form of a cashier's check along with your official id. Any excess funds will be issued to you immediately.

Move in and stay in! Move in your new home and don't try to "keep up with the Jones'"! Maintain your budget and live within your means. Utilize bonuses, tax refunds, and other additional cash flow to improve your property and increase your six-month savings and emergency fund. Save separately for new furniture and pay for it with cash if and only if you have the rest of your financial house in order! If you are going to miss a mortgage payment, reach out to your lender or a HUD-approved counselor right away to discuss options.

FAQS: GET YOUR CREDIT IN ORDER!

Q: How do I establish credit to purchase a

home if I don't have any credit cards or loans?

A: You can use a service called "Pay Rent Build Credit" www.prbc.com, which uses non-traditional forms of credit such as: cell phones, utilities, child support, and alimony to establish a credit report separate from Equifax, Experian and TransUnion. This nontraditional credit report can be used to help get approved for a mortgage loan under the FHA and VA mortgage guidelines. You can also get a secured credit card and request that the account be reported to the 3 major credit bureaus: Equifax, Experian and TransUnion.

Q: If I file for bankruptcy can I still be approved for a mortgage loan?

A: Yes, but you may receive a higher interest

rate and may not get the best deal. Although you can receive a market interest rate FHA mortgage while you are still paying off a chapter 13 bankruptcy (as long as you have been paying on time for at least one year and have no other negative credit since the bankruptcy) and one year after the discharge of a chapter 7 bankruptcy (if the bankruptcy was filed due to an uncontrollable circumstance like death, divorce, or medical illness), most programs require that you wait two years before applying for a mortgage loan and many require that you wait for four years. Following my Mortgage Approval Plan will assist you along your path to homeownership. It is important to remember to pay all of your bills on time after a bankruptcy if you wish to get approved for a mortgage in the   future.

Q: How do I fix errors on my credit report and get approved for a mortgage?
A: Get an updated copy of your credit report every three months during the first year after your bankruptcy. Review everything and report everything that is not correct. Send a dispute letter to the credit bureau reporting the error and provide any documentation to support your claim that incorrect information has been reported. You can also dispute the information online at each credit bureau's website (Equifax, Experian and TransUnion).

During the mortgage application process, you may also request that your loan officer obtain a

Residential Mortgage Credit Report (RMCR) to submit to the underwriter with your mortgage application. The RMCR will provide a quick update of the incorrect information and allow the underwriter to see what your credit report would like in its improved state. The RMCR is also a quick way to have non-traditional credit lines (like rent, utility payments, cell phone payments, child support payments, etc.) added to your credit report in the event you have little or no credit. You may also request a "re-score" (resulting in a higher credit score and possibly a better loan and interest rate) along with the RMCR for a fee.

Q: How long does negative information stay on my credit report?

A: Most negative information (late payments or unpaid bills) can appear on your credit report for 7 years. Bankruptcies and unpaid judgments can remain for 7 to 10 years. Unpaid tax liens (government taxes owed on earned income or on a house, car or other asset) can remain for up to 7 years or more.

Q: What should I do if I am applying for a mortgage but my credit has been negatively impacted as a result of identity theft?

A: If someone steals your identity and opens an account in your name without your knowledge, you should contact a professional identity theft service but you should also do the following:

- Contact the company and close the affected account and open a new one. If the account required a PIN create a new one.

- Contact the credit bureaus and ask to speak to someone in the Fraud Department.

- Request a security alert which alerts creditors to confirm the consumer's identity before extending credit.

- Request that your name be removed from prescreened credit offer lists.

- Request a copy of your credit report.

- File a police report.

- Contact the companies you do business with and inform them that you have been a victim of identity theft.

- Contact your local post office and inform them you have been a victim of identity theft.

- Contact your local Social Security Administration office and inform them you have been a victim of identity theft.

- Save all written documentation above to submit with your mortgage application. You will need extensive evidence to yield a mortgage approval if identity theft has negativity impacted your credit report.

Q: A collection agency contacted me about a 10-year-old debt. Do I still have to pay it?

A: Check to see if the statute of limitations (time period a company has available to pursue collecting a debt) has expired. If it has expired, you are not legally obligated to pay the debt and it should be removed from your credit report. If it has not expired, then the company is still able to pursue and accordingly, you must set up a payment plan to pay the debt. http://www.creditinfocenter.com/rebuild/statuteLimitations.shtml#2

FAQS: GET YOUR MORTGAGE IN ORDER!

Q: I am putting down less than 20 percent and my loan requires private mortgage insurance. Will I have to pay this forever?
A: No. When you have more than 20% equity

in your home, mortgage insurance is no longer required. Let's look at this example. If your home is valued at $100,000 at the time of purchase, then you are eligible to have your mortgage insurance removed when the balance is less than $80,000. Conversely, if your home increases in value, and your balance is less than 80% of the new value, then you should contact your lender and request an appraisal from a licensed appraiser that is approved by your lender, in order to substantiate your new value and potentially have your private mortgage insurance removed from your payment.

Q: I am a first time homebuyer. What down payment assistance programs are available?

A: There are hundreds, possibly thousands of

programs available to first time homebuyers, many vary by state, and some are even available to those who are not purchasing real estate for the first time, as long as the buyer intends to live in the property. Trying to find a program without an adequate analysis from a seasoned mortgage professional is like calling the doctor with a cough and wanting to know if you have a cold or cancer! The doctor must take your bloodwork if you want a proper diagnosis. Likewise, your lender will need to obtain extensive pertinent details about you in order to properly diagnose you with the down payment assistance program and mortgage that is best for you.

Q. The property I have chosen needs repairs

but I am a first time homebuyer with limited cash. Is there help for me?

A: Yes, the Federal Housing Administration FHA 203(k) Rehabilitation loan may be the answer to your prayers. With this loan, you can roll the cost of minor repairs under a certain dollar amount into the Streamline (K) loan and the cost of major repairs and renovations into the regular 203(k) loan. In addition, you can convert a 4 unit building into a 2 unit or vice versa, and you can use this program to acquire mixed use property (residential area combined with commercial space such as a beauty shop, day care facility, etc) and maximize your cash flow by living upstairs in the residential portion and having your business downstairs in the commercial portion of the building.

http://www.hud.gov/offices/hsg/sfh/203k/203kmenu.cfm

Q: I am a veteran. What options are available for me?

A: The VA loan program is an excellent option because it requires no down payment, has no mortgage insurance, and like the FHA loan, requires no minimum credit score (though there are credit guidelines that must be adhered to). Moreover, the VA loan can be used to acquire 1 – 4 unit properties and the spouse of an active duty veteran can purchase real estate while the active duty veteran is overseas.

FAQS: GET YOUR LEGAL ISSUES IN ORDER!

Q: Should I purchase real estate with my significant other (or sibling / friend / business partner,   etc.)?

A: You should be careful when mixing business with pleasure!!! Purchasing real estate is just that: a business transaction. Despite popular belief, marriage actually affords individuals a legal benefit to share in the assets acquired during the course of the marriage and in some states, it also includes those items acquired prior to the marriage and brought into the marriage and maintained by both parties during the course of the marriage in some form or fashion. Therefore if you "must" purchase real estate with any joint owner, then you "must" follow these rules:

1. Ensure that both of your names appear on the title of the property at some point only after the following nine (9) points have been completed. If you fail to complete 2-10, you cannot do #1.

2. Determine the legal manner in which title will be taken (i.e., joint tenancy or tenants-in-common) if both of your names will appear on title. For example, if upon your death you want your share of the property to pass to your children or your heirs instead of to the joint owner of the property, you would hold the property as "tenants-in-common." If you want

your share to go "only" to the joint owner, then "joint tenancy" would be your best choice. (Check with your local real estate attorney regarding your state's applicable laws)

3. Talk to a real estate attorney (not a criminal/civil/accident/etc. attorney) to sort out the options available in your state and decide what should occur with each of your respective shares if you were to become disabled, terminally ill or if you pass away.

4. Find out if either party is currently married or is currently going through a divorce. (You might find yourself in a legal battle with your significant other's spouse who he/she failed to discuss with you.)

5. Make sure you are aware of all of the children of your joint owner/significant other (the real estate might become subject to litigation in a child support proceeding).

6. Have your joint owner provide a current copy of his/her credit report. (Note: all judgments and tax liens will attach to the real estate when real property is transferred via a Quit Claim Deed. Therefore if your joint owner has a judgment for an outstanding child support matter or any other matter, that lien will automatically attach to the real estate that you now own together).

7. Develop a plan for the real estate in case either of you elect to not remain in the

relationship / partnership / friendship.

8. Have a minimum of six (6) months of full mortgage payments saved (not just your share) in case of an emergency / break-up / argument or other unfortunate event.

9. Determine the roles that you will have with respect to the real estate. Who will maintain the property, who will pay the bills associated with the property, etc.?

10. Write your answers to questions 2-9 and then answer question #1. IF AND ONLY IF all answers to questions 1-10 are in writing, should you then consider purchasing property with a friend / business partner / significant other that you are not legally married to; and even for

married couples, this is a good thing to have.

Q: If the Seller verbally promises in front of others to complete certain repairs and later decides at closing not to make the repairs, is the Seller liable? Can I make him complete the repairs as promised since I have witnesses?
A: If the promise is not in writing and it relates to real estate, it is typically not enforceable. Therefore you must check with an attorney in your area, but in most instances, you will not be able to enforce the verbal promise.

FAQS: GET YOUR INSURANCE IN ORDER!

Q: How much does homeowner's insurance cost?

A: The price of a homeowner's insurance policy is determined by several factors. The age of the property, size of the property, inside amenities, location and type of construction are examples of the different factors that can affect the price. Unless there are uniquely extreme market conditions, a homebuyer should budget $600 to $1000 for the annual cost of a homeowner's insurance policy.

Q: What is replacement cost coverage?

A: Replacement cost coverage looks to restore a homeowner back to her original state when a loss is experienced. Replacement cost coverage looks to give you what it would cost in today's dollars to replace the physical property that was lost or damaged. Replacement cost coverage in a homeowner's policy is the superior coverage because it protects the homeowner from receiving a depreciated or actual cash value settlement in the event of a claim.

Q: Does my homeowner's policy protect me against floods?

A: The homeowner's insurance policy will protect you against named perils. Fire, lightning, theft, vandalism and wind are some of the more common instances that are covered under the policy. Flood protection is NOT covered under the basic homeowner's insurance policy. A flood policy is a separate federally sponsored insurance policy. If the area where your home is located is within a flood zone (or an area that historically is plagued by flooding) AND if there is a mortgage on the property, the mortgage company will require you to purchase a separate flood insurance policy.

Go forth and prosper! Building wealth is like building a great relationship: you must give them honest and loving attention if you want them to grow.

Journaling Your Way to Love & Prosperity:
Now it's your turn to write: What is your
current credit score, credit challenges, and real
estate goals in your relationship?

_____

_____

_____

_____

_____

_____

_____

_____

_____

_____

_____

_____

_____

_____

Journaling Your Way to Love & Prosperity:
Now it's your turn to write: What real property
does each of you own and what changes do
you need to make?

_____

_____

_____

_____

_____

_____

_____

_____

_____

_____

_____

_____

About   MC   Lyte

Lyricist, pioneer, icon, inspirational speaker, veteran, philanthropist, and entrepreneur describe one of the most prolific and well-respected female Hip Hop artists of our time: **Lana "MC Lyte" Moorer.** A pioneer in the industry, she opened the door for future female Hip Hop artists by daring to do what had never been done while doing something she loved. A role model to women and respected by men everywhere, Lyte never compromises who she is and consistently displays that a woman can turn heads fully clothed! Whenever possible, **Lyte,** as she is affectionately known by her inner circle, enjoys traveling across the nation to use her expertise and story of success to motivate others to take ownership of the world around them while striving to be the best they can possibly be. Author of "**Unstoppable: Igniting the Power Within to Achieve Your Greatest Potential**," "**Living in the Lyte: Lessons in Life, Love and Truth**" and co-author of "**Fusion: Bridging the Gap Between Civil Rights and Hip Hop**," **MC Lyte** is also very active in many social projects, including anti-violence campaigns and Rock the Vote. **MC Lyte** is the Founder/Chairman of Hip Hop Sisters Foundation, Inc. the CEO of Sunni Gyrl, Inc., a past President of the Los Angeles Chapter of the Recording Academy (Grammy Organization), and she is also a proud honorary member of Sigma Gamma Rho Sorority, Inc.

About Lynn Richardson

Named by Urban Influence Magazine as one of the 20 Hottest Influencers in America, *Dr. Lynn Richardson, also known as the Madea of Money,* is a Chaplain, television personality, author, entertainment executive and celebrity financial coach who uses her quick wit and humorous presentation style to help others face their money issues and achieve personal, professional and spiritual harmony. With more than two decades of leading roles in the banking and real estate sales industries, Lynn vision is best portrayed in her books, most notably Living Check to Monday: The Real Deal About Money, Credit and Financial Security, which achieved Best Seller status at the 2008 Congressional Black Caucus Conference Book Pavilion. Lynn is featured regularly on the BET & Centric Networks and has appeared in Essence, Jet, Upscale, on the Tom Joyner Morning Show, and in countless media outlets nationwide. She has served as Chief of Operations for Russell Simmons' and Dr. Benjamin Chavis' Hip Hop Summit Action Network and is currently the President and CEO of MC Lyte's Hip Hop Sisters Foundation, President and COO of MC Lyte's Sunni Gyrl entertainment and celebrity management firm, and where she oversees entertainment and empowerment strategies that impact the globe.

Join the Movement:
www.hiphopsisters.org

About Hip-Hop Sisters Foundation
Founded by MC Lyte, the legendary lyricist and iconic hip-hop pioneer, Hip Hop Sisters Foundation is a non-profit organization that promotes positive images of women of ethnic diversity, bringing leaders from the world of Hip Hop, the entertainment industry, and the corporate world.

Celebrity advisory board members include Faith Evans, Ledisi, Jada Pinkett Smith, Chilli, Russell Simmons, Cheryl "Salt" James, Malinda Williams, Kelly Price, Malcolm Jamal Warner, and Dr. Benjamin Chavis.

Join us at
The W.E.A.L.T.H. Experience
www.wealthexperience.info